Symbols of American Freedom

The Lincoln Memorial

by Chelsey Hankins

Series Consultant: Jerry D. Thompson,
Regents Professor of History,
Texas A&M International University

CHELSEA CLUBHOUSE

An Imprint of Chelsea House Publishers

Symbols of American Freedom: The Lincoln Memorial

Chelsea Clubhouse
An imprint of Chelsea House Publishers
132 West 31st Street
New York NY 10001

Library of Congress Cataloging-in-Publication Data
Hankins, Chelsey.
    The Lincoln Memorial / by Chelsey Hankins.
        p. cm. — (Symbols of American freedom)
    Includes index.
    ISBN 978-1-60413-518-3
    1. Lincoln Memorial (Washington, D.C.)—Juvenile literature. 2. Lincoln, Abraham, 1809-1865—Monuments—Washington (D.C.)—Juvenile literature. 3. Lincoln, Abraham, 1809-1865—Juvenile literature. 4. Washington (D.C.)—Buildings, structures, etc.—Juvenile literature. I. Title. II. Series.
    F203.4.L73H36 2009
    975.3—dc22
                                        2009012176

Developed for Chelsea House by RJF Publishing LLC (www.RJFpublishing.com)
Text and cover design by Tammy West/Westgraphix LLC
Maps by Stefan Chabluk
Photo research by Edward A. Thomas
Index by Nila Glikin

Photo Credits: 5: Library of Congress (LOC) Rep #LC-DIG-ppmsca-19301; 6, 32: iStockphoto; 7: AP/Wide World Photos; 9: © Flip Schulke/CORBIS; 11: LOC Rep # LC-USZC4-2472; 13: LOC Rep# LC-USZC4-6189; 14, 25: Peter Newark American Pictures/The Bridgeman Art Library; 16: National Park Service; 19: LOC Rep# LC-USZ62-136306; 20: LOC Rep# LC-DIG-ppmsca-19520; 24: LOC Rep# LC-DIG-pga-02502; 26: LOC Rep# LC-USZ61-903; 27: LOC Rep# LC-USZ62-2280; 28: New-York Historical Society/The Bridgeman Art Library; 31: LOC Rep# LC-USZ62-77389; 35: LOC Rep# LC-USZ62-96487; 37: © ClassicStock/Alamy; 39: U.S. Mint; 41: © Edward A. Thomas; 43: © Directphoto.org/Alamy.

Note: Quotations in the text are used essentially as originally written. In some cases, spelling, punctuation, and the like have been modernized to aid student understanding.

Table of Contents

Words that are defined in the Glossary are in **bold** type
the first time they appear in the text.

The Importance of the Lincoln Memorial

Abraham Lincoln is often considered the greatest president in the history of the United States. Lincoln led the United States during the Civil War (1861–1865). He worked to save the **Union**—that is, to keep the United States one country. He took action to end the practice of slavery. He always paid attention to the needs of the country even during times of personal crisis, such as the death of his young son Willie in 1862.

Lincoln's presidency ended with his **assassination**, or murder, in April 1865. Lincoln was killed just as the Civil War was ending with a Union victory. He will forever be remembered as the president who led the country through one of its darkest hours.

Remembering Lincoln

To remember Lincoln's life and presidency, a national **memorial** was built in Washington, D.C. The Lincoln Memorial was completed

This photograph of President Abraham Lincoln was taken in November 1863, while Lincoln was leading the country through the Civil War.

in 1922. Today, it is one of many historical **monuments** located on the **National Mall**, a long, tree-lined plaza that runs between the memorial and the Capitol building, where Congress meets. The memorial includes a marble statue of Lincoln inside a rectangular stone building. The statue shows Lincoln seated in a chair. He is looking out across the Mall to the Capitol and the nearby Washington Monument, which honors President

Facts About the Lincoln Memorial

Height of Lincoln's statue	19 feet (6 meters)
Weight of Lincoln's statue (including the base)	175 tons (159 metric tons)
Height of the building's 36 columns	44 feet (13 meters)
Height of the building	79 feet 10 inches (24 meters)

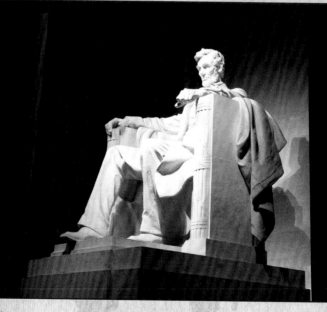

The statue of Abraham Lincoln inside the Lincoln Memorial is 19 feet high.

George Washington. Visitors can walk up the steps and go inside the memorial building to get closer to the statue. They can look out at the Reflecting Pool, which is a large pool of water in front of the memorial.

Standing at the top of the steps leading into the Lincoln Memorial, singer Marian Anderson gives a concert in April 1939. She sang there after she was not allowed to perform at a concert hall because she was black.

There are several reasons why Washington, D.C., is a fitting location for a memorial to Abraham Lincoln. He and his family lived in the White House in Washington while he served as president. Washington, D.C., is also the location of other presidential memorials. Memorials were also built there in honor of Franklin D. Roosevelt and Thomas Jefferson.

An Important Gathering Place

The Lincoln Memorial has often served as a gathering place for important events. Many years after the Civil War ended, African Americans were still not treated equally. In 1939, an African-American singer named Marian Anderson was not allowed to sing at a concert hall in Washington, D.C., because she was black. Eleanor Roosevelt was the wife of Franklin D. Roosevelt, who was president at the time. When she heard about this, she quickly arranged for Anderson to sing on the steps of the Lincoln Memorial instead.

In Their Own Words

Martin Luther King's "I Have a Dream" Speech

Martin Luther King Jr. was an important leader in the civil rights movement of the 1950s and 1960s. He was also one of several people who spoke at the 1963 March on Washington. His speech is probably the best remembered because of its simple theme—the dream of a better world:

> "I have a dream that one day on the red hills of Georgia the sons of former slaves and the sons of former slave owners will be able to sit down together at the table of brotherhood. I have a dream that one day even the state of Mississippi, a state sweltering with the heat of injustice, sweltering with the heat of oppression, will be transformed into an oasis of freedom and justice. I have a dream that my four little children will one day live in a nation where they will not be judged by the color of their skin but by the content of their character. I have a dream today."

The positive tone of King's speech helped to encourage African Americans around the country to continue to stand up for their rights.

During the **civil rights movement** of the 1950s and 1960s, the Lincoln Memorial was an important place for people working for equal rights for African Americans. In 1963, thousands of African Americans and other people gathered in front of the memorial and along the sides of the Reflecting Pool. They were there for the March on Washington. The march was their way of sending a message to the country that African Americans were tired of being treated poorly and not having equal rights. At one point during the march, the civil rights leader Martin Luther King Jr. spoke from the top of the memorial's steps. King gave a famous speech called the "I Have a Dream" speech.

Many thousands of people gathered in front of the Lincoln Memorial and around the Reflecting Pool in 1963 to hear Martin Luther King Jr.'s "I Have a Dream" speech.

A few years later, when the United States was involved in the Vietnam War, thousands of demonstrators again gathered around the Lincoln Memorial to protest. They wanted the president, Lyndon B. Johnson, to end the war. These protestors gathered at the Lincoln Memorial because it was close enough to the White House to get the president's attention.

Lincoln's Early Life and Career

Abraham Lincoln was born on February 12, 1809, in a log cabin in Kentucky. When he was seven, his family moved to southwestern Indiana. In those days, Kentucky and Indiana were still considered to be close to the American **frontier**. This was an imaginary line separating the states in the East, which were more completely settled, from the West, which was still being explored and settled.

Abraham's family had to live off the land. They hunted, fished, and raised their food instead of buying it in a store. Abraham rarely got to attend school. His mother gave him most of his early education.

Working Hard and Teaching Himself

The Lincoln family dealt with many struggles as Abraham was growing up. His little brother, Thomas, died as a baby. His mother died when Abraham was only nine. Although his father worked hard, the family was always very

This picture shows Abraham Lincoln as a young man splitting logs—that is, cutting them into smaller pieces of wood that could be used for fence rails, firewood, and other things. Frontier life meant hard work for Lincoln and all the other members of his family.

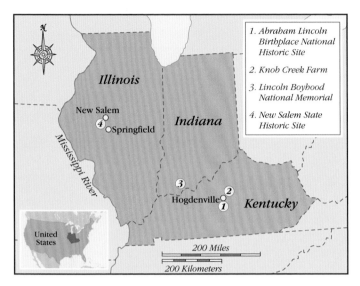

1. Abraham Lincoln Birthplace National Historic Site

2. Knob Creek Farm

3. Lincoln Boyhood National Memorial

4. New Salem State Historic Site

Several places where Lincoln lived as a child or young adult are now historic sites that people can visit.

poor. Abraham worked hard in order to help his father, but he also spent some of his time teaching himself what he did not get to learn in school. By the time he was an adult, he had taught himself most of what he knew—including grammar and math—by using books borrowed from other people. He sometimes walked for miles just to borrow a book. His favorite books were adventure stories.

Abraham was 21 years old when the family decided to move again, this time to central Illinois. By that time, Abraham was tall and strong. He was 6 feet 4 inches (2 meters) tall and very thin, but his arms and legs were strong from his hard work helping around the farm and cutting firewood with an axe. From living for so long in the backwoods of Kentucky and Indiana, Abraham had a country accent that instantly told people where he was from.

Lincoln did not want to follow in his father's footsteps and become a farmer. After the family moved to Illinois, he took a job on a boat that traveled up and down the Mississippi River. He then worked briefly as a storekeeper and a postmaster in the village of New Salem, outside of Springfield, Illinois. What Lincoln really wanted to be, though, was a lawyer. He studied law books and passed an exam in order to become a lawyer.

Mary Todd Lincoln (1818–1882)

Mary Todd was born in 1818 into a wealthy family in Lexington, Kentucky. She grew up around slavery because Kentucky was a slave state. In fact, her family owned slaves. Mary's later beliefs that slavery was wrong were very different from the beliefs she grew up with. When she was 21, Mary decided to move to Springfield, Illinois, to live with her sister and brother-in-law. In Springfield, Mary met and began dating Abraham Lincoln. She was a popular girl, and many men wanted to date her. Because Lincoln was still just a country lawyer at the time, Mary's family tried to talk her out of marrying him. They were worried that he would not make a good enough husband for a wealthy girl from Lexington. Little did Mary's family know that her husband would one day become the president of the United States.

A Lawyer and a Politician

Lincoln moved to Springfield in 1837 to open an office and begin making his living as a lawyer. Although he had grown up poor, he now made good money as a lawyer. In Springfield, Lincoln met Mary Todd. They were married in 1842, and their first son, Robert, was born a year later.

In the 1830s, Lincoln decided to become a politician. He decided to run for a seat in the Illinois state **legislature**. He wanted to be a lawmaker because he thought he had many good ideas for helping his state. Lincoln believed it was important for the government to pay for building railroads, roadways, and canals, especially in frontier states like Illinois. He thought it was important to link Illinois and areas beyond it on the western frontier with the rest of the United States. He once said that the goal of government "is to do for a community of people whatever they need to have done, but cannot do at all, or cannot do so well, for themselves." He served in the

Slavery in America

Millions of African slaves had been brought to the New World from the 1500s to the 1800s. These slaves were carried across the Atlantic Ocean on large boats where conditions were very crowded and dirty. Many people died of disease, starvation, and poor treatment on this long voyage. In large cities like New Orleans, Louisiana; Atlanta, Georgia; and Washington, D.C., slaves worked in homes as cooks, housekeepers, butlers, and drivers. In many parts of the South, slaves lived on large **plantations**. There, they were forced to work long hours in the fields, planting and harvesting such crops as cotton. While their masters lived in large, comfortable homes, slaves typically lived in cabins on the edge of the property. They had very little furniture and few personal items. No one could tell masters how to treat their slaves. No one could pre-vent masters from treating slaves cruelly. Instead of being considered

people, slaves were considered property. They could be sold from one master to another. Family members could be sold separately. When this happened, parents and children or husbands and wives might never see each other again. By 1861, there were about 4 mil-lion slaves living in the American South.

Lincoln (in the white jacket) debates slavery with Stephen Douglas during their 1858 Senate campaign in Illinois.

state legislature from 1834 to 1840. Later, he served in the U.S. Congress from 1847 to 1849.

The Slavery Issue

As early as the 1830s, Lincoln showed his support for **abolitionists**, people who wanted to abolish, or end, slavery. Most people in the southern states thought that the government did not have the right to restrict slavery. There were many large farms, called plantations, in the South, and plantation owners used slave labor to grow their crops. Plantations did not exist in the North, so it was harder for northerners to understand why slavery should be allowed. Many people in the North wanted to make slavery illegal. By the 1850s, members of Congress and other leaders from the North and the South often had heated arguments about this issue.

Lincoln became well known across the country when he decided to run for the U.S. Senate in the 1858 elections. He ran as the candidate of the Republican Party in the state of Illinois. He wanted the Senate seat that was held by a politician named Stephen Douglas, who was a member of the Democratic Party. Douglas believed that individual states and **territories** should decide whether to allow slavery or not. He supported allowing slavery to spread to territories such as Kansas and Nebraska, which were getting ready to become states. Lincoln, however, was strongly opposed to this spread of slavery. Lincoln had hated the practice of one human being owning another ever since he first saw slavery in Kentucky.

He decided it was important for him to speak out about these issues as a U.S. senator. At the Republican Party **convention** in Springfield, Lincoln gave his famous "A House Divided" speech. In it, he talked about the future problems of the nation if people disagreed about slavery:

> "I believe this government cannot endure, permanently half slave and half free…. It will become all one thing, or all the other."

Other Lincoln Sites

In addition to the Lincoln Memorial, there are several other historic sites where visitors can learn more about Lincoln's life. The Abraham Lincoln Birthplace National Historic Site is made up of two places in Kentucky (including Knob Creek Farm). Visitors can see cabins similar to the ones the Lincoln family would have lived in when Abraham was a young boy. The Lincoln Boyhood National Memorial in Indiana is dedicated to the 14 years Lincoln spent there. The memorial is located on the same site where the Lincoln farm was located. It is also near the grave of Lincoln's mother. Yet another place is the New Salem State Historic Site in Illinois, which is a reconstruction of the village where Lincoln lived as a young adult. It contains a general store, a blacksmith shop, a mill, and many small houses that look similar to the ones that were present in the town when Lincoln lived there.

As a boy, Lincoln lived with his family in a tiny cabin such as this one, which can be seen at Knob Creek Farm in Kentucky.

Lincoln did not think the country could last much longer if the states disagreed about slavery. At the same time, he did not believe that states had a right to choose to leave the Union.

Lincoln asked Douglas to appear with him in a series of **debates** so that they could talk about these issues in front of an audience. Lincoln lost the election to Douglas. The debates, however, made Lincoln famous throughout the nation.

Elected to the Presidency

Lincoln became the Republican candidate for president in the election of 1860. The Republican Party's main competition was the Democratic Party, which supported allowing people in the new territories to decide slavery issues for themselves. Although the Democratic Party was favored to win the election, something unusual happened in that year: The party split. Some people in the party supported one candidate, Douglas, while other people supported another candidate, Vice President John Breckinridge. A fourth candidate, John Bell, was also running.

When all of the votes were counted, Lincoln had won the election. More people had voted against him than voted for him, but the votes against him were split among the three other candidates. Many people who favored slavery or who thought the government should not stop the expansion of slavery in new states were very angry that Lincoln had won.

The Votes for President in 1860	
Candidate	**Votes**
Abraham Lincoln	1,865,908 (45%)
Stephen Douglas	848,019 (21%)
John Breckinridge	845,763 (20%)
John Bell	589,581 (14%)
Total Vote	**4,149,271 (100%)**

Chapter 3

President Lincoln

The Lincoln family moved from their home in Springfield to the White House in early 1861. Washington, D.C., was a very different city back then from what it is today, and the White House was different, too. In the summer, the hot, humid weather made the White House—which like all buildings had no air conditioning—very uncomfortable for the Lincolns. The building also had no modern plumbing, and the family sometimes got sick from drinking unclean water that came from the nearby Potomac River. The river also often smelled bad during hot summer weather, and the smell filled the White House.

Another big difference in the White House was that it had no security guards or locked gates. The president's house was seen as a public home, where the door should always be open to people who wanted to meet with him. Mary Lincoln was often annoyed that there were always people in the White House

This photograph shows the White House in the 1860s, at about the time that Lincoln and his family lived there.

hoping to catch a glimpse of her husband and family. Mary tried to decorate the house with fashionable rugs, vases, and dishes, but visitors often tracked dirt onto the rugs. Visitors also stole items like dishes because they wanted to have a souvenir from the White House.

Sometimes, the Lincoln boys were not much better than the public. When they moved into the White House, the president and his wife had three sons—Robert, Tad, and Willie. (A fourth son, Eddie, had died in 1850.) Although Robert was away at Harvard University for most of the time his father was president, Tad and Willie lived with their parents in the White House. Many visitors would complain that the boys—who sometimes let their pet goats run through the house—were too wild and playful.

The Beginning of the Civil War

Lincoln had very little time to worry about guests in the White House or his sons' behavior. Soon after he was elected president in November 1860, some southern states had decided to **secede** from, or leave, the Union. The

Political Cartoons

Beginning during the presidential election of 1860, newspaper editors published political cartoons that made fun of Lincoln. Throughout his presidency, he would be confronted by drawings of himself. The drawings exaggerated the appearance of his body, made fun of his views on slavery, and laughed at his rural upbringing.

leaders of these states believed Lincoln's victory meant an end to their way of life. Lincoln tried to convince them that this was not so, but they did not believe him. They wanted nothing to do with the country if Abraham Lincoln was the president.

The Civil War began when Confederate forces fired bombs at Fort Sumter, South Carolina, on April 12, 1861. As a result of the heavy bombardment, the fort's defenders surrendered the next day.

The first state to leave the Union was South Carolina in December 1860. In January and February 1861, Mississippi, Florida, Alabama, Georgia, Louisiana, and Texas seceded. On February 9, southern states formed the Confederate States of America, often just called the Confederacy. The Confederates chose Jefferson Davis, a slave owner who had served as secretary of war under President Franklin Pierce, to be their new president.

The Civil War began on April 12, 1861, when Confederate forces fired on Fort Sumter, which is on an island in the harbor at Charleston, South Carolina. Their actions sent a clear message that the Confederate states were serious about separating from the Union permanently. Days after the attack on Fort Sumter, Virginia seceded. In May, Arkansas, Tennessee, and North Carolina did, too. After Virginia joined the Confederacy, the city of Richmond, Virginia, became the Confederate capital. Richmond was only about 100 miles (160 kilometers) from Washington, D.C.

Lincoln knew that despite his best efforts to keep the country at peace, war had begun. The North would have to fight to defeat the Confederate states and bring them back into the Union. He was deeply saddened by the outbreak of the Civil War. His only comfort was his belief that the war would not last long. There were twice as many Union states as Confederate states, and the Union had twice as many people as the Confederacy. It seemed impossible that the Confederacy would be able to keep the Union from victory for very long.

Border States in the Union

Although most of the slave states joined the Confederacy, some did not. Missouri, Kentucky, Maryland, and Delaware all allowed slavery when the Civil War began, but they chose to remain loyal to the Union. These border states were located next to the Confederacy and close to much of the conflict. They provided critical help to the Union during the war.

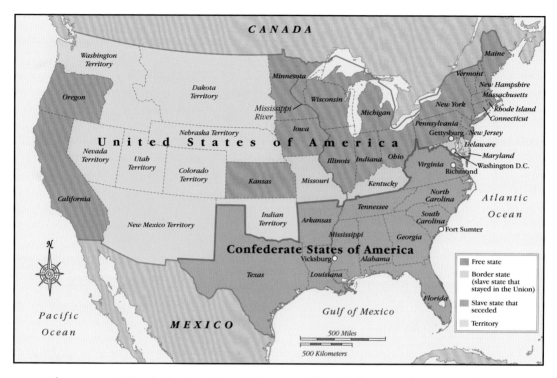

There were 11 Confederate states at the start of the Civil War and 23 states that stayed in the Union, including four border states that allowed slavery but did not secede.

The Early Years of the War

Lincoln called for 75,000 volunteers to serve in the Union Army at the start of the war, and men from all over the North answered his call. They joined army **regiments** made up of other men from their hometowns and nearby communities. They received training on how to fight and how to fire a gun. The lowest-level Union soldiers were paid about $12 per month—a lot of money back then—and many states gave additional bonuses to men who joined the army.

In the summer of 1861, Union and Confederate soldiers met in the first large battle of the war. The battle took place at Manassas Junction, Virginia. (It is sometimes called the Battle of Bull Run, because a stream called Bull Run was nearby.) The Confederates beat the Union soldiers, sending fear through northern leaders back in Washington that the South might be harder to defeat than they had thought. Quickly, Lincoln named George McClellan—a West Point graduate, politician, and railroad president—to be in charge of the Union Army near Washington, called the Army of the Potomac. Lincoln hoped that McClellan's leadership would turn things around.

In 1861 and 1862, Union and Confederate armies met in battle in such places as Louisiana, Tennessee, Virginia, and Maryland. The biggest surprise of these battles was that, especially in Virginia, the North was losing so many of them. Reports of bloody, deadly battles reached Washington. Frustrated with the how long the war had already lasted, Lincoln began to consider other ways to weaken the South.

The Emancipation Proclamation

Lincoln always thought slavery was wrong, but when he ran for president he did not say that he would end slavery in the South—he would just keep it out of new states. When the Civil War began, he said the North was fighting the South just to restore the Union and not to end slavery. As the war went on and so many soldiers died, though, Lincoln decided that the war should also have the goal of ending slavery. He also had other reasons for wanting to free the slaves. One reason was that slaves were helping the southern war effort. Union Army leaders told him that if slaves in the South knew they could be free by escaping to areas controlled by Union troops, many slaves would do that and work for the Union Army.

Lincoln was also worried that Great Britain and other countries in Europe would recognize the Confederacy as a new nation. Then, Britain might send weapons and other supplies to the Confederates. Britain, however, had ended its slave trade in 1807, and people in Britain did not like the practice of slavery. Lincoln believed that if one of the Union goals in the Civil War became ending slavery, Britain would not back the Confederates.

This picture shows Lincoln discussing an early version of the Emancipation Proclamation at the White House with his advisers in 1862.

Many people in the North did not understand why Lincoln wanted to take action to free slaves in the South. They constantly criticized him for making what they thought was a very unwise decision. Lincoln's advisers suggested that he should wait before taking action against slavery. The North had been losing battle after battle in the war. The advisers suggested that Lincoln should wait for a clear Union victory.

On September 17, 1862, he got that victory in the Battle of Antietam. In this battle, fought in Maryland, Union troops stopped a Confederate army that was moving north. Five days later, on September 22, Lincoln made an important announcement. He said that he would free the slaves in all areas that were rebelling against the United States unless the Confederate states came back into the Union by January 1, 1863. This was an early version of the **Emancipation** Proclamation. Lincoln issued the final Emancipation

The Death of Willie Lincoln

Willie Lincoln came down with a fever in early 1862. He probably had a disease called typhoid fever, which he could have gotten from drinking the unclean water at the White House. Willie got worse and worse, and he died on February 20, 1862, at the age of 11. The Lincolns were devastated by the death of their son. Mary's **seamstress**, who was in the room when President Lincoln first heard of his son's death, later wrote that the president "buried his head in his hands, and his tall frame was convulsed with emotion. I stood at the foot of the bed, my eyes full of tears, looking at the man in silent, awe-stricken wonder. His grief unnerved him, and made him a weak passive child." Even though he was still very upset about Willie's death, Lincoln had to go back to work, planning for the war, after only a few days of mourning. Mary, though, found it difficult to go on with her daily life because she was so sad. She was upset about Willie's death for the rest of her life.

Proclamation on January 1, 1863. Since the Emancipation Proclamation ended slavery only in areas outside Union control, it had little power to free slaves until the war was over. Some slaves, though, did escape and help the Union Army. And the Emancipation Proclamation became an important **symbol** of one of the things the Union was now fighting for.

The War Continues

The Union Army continued to lose battles, so Lincoln made changes in the Army's leadership. In late 1862, he decided to fire General McClellan. He thought that McClellan was not fighting hard enough for the Union. He wanted a general who would lead his troops boldly to victory. First, Lincoln replaced McClellan with Ambrose Burnside. Then he replaced Burnside with "Fighting Joe" Hooker. Then he replaced Hooker with George Meade. Meade was in command during one of the bloodiest battles of the Civil War—where the tide began to turn for the Union.

This was the Battle of Gettysburg, which took place in Pennsylvania during the first three days of July 1863. Together, the Union and the Confederacy lost more than 50,000 soldiers killed or wounded in the long battle. Gettysburg was an important Union victory. Meade's army stopped the Confederates from advancing farther north. The victory raised the spirits of people in the North and made them more determined to keep on fighting. The Confederates' defeat also made it less likely that Britain would come to the aid of the South.

A cemetery for the Union soldiers killed in the battle was dedicated at Gettysburg on November 19, 1863. President Lincoln attended the ceremony, and he gave a short speech. That speech has become known as the Gettysburg Address. Many people think it was the greatest speech of his career. He honored the soldiers who had given their lives to preserve the Union and also encouraged his soldiers to continue fighting.

General Ulysses S. Grant became commander of all the Union armies in 1864.

Reelection and the End of the Civil War

In the November 1864 election, Lincoln was re-elected as president. People believed the Union was going to win the war, so they wanted Lincoln to be president for the next four years. By then, Lincoln had named Ulysses S. Grant as the commander of all the Union forces.

The Civil War continued to drag on throughout 1864 and the spring of 1865, even though it had become obvious that the

This photograph of Lincoln with his son Tad was taken in early 1865. Many people thought Lincoln looked much older in 1865 than he had when he first became president just four years earlier.

Union would win. The Confederates had run out of money. They were running out of men for the army. Parts of the South had been largely destroyed by the many battles that had taken place there. The Union Army had several key victories. The Union took over southern cities such as Atlanta and Savannah in Georgia, and finally the Confederate capital of Richmond. Then, the Confederates' top general, Robert E. Lee, felt he had no choice. He surrendered to General Grant on April 9, 1865. In the weeks that followed, other Confederate generals surrendered as well. In all, half a million soldiers had died during the Civil War, more than in any other war in American history.

Lincoln felt relieved when the South surrendered. The fighting that had killed so many young men was finally over. The Union was saved, and slavery would end. At Lincoln's urging, in 1865, Congress and the states approved the Thirteenth Amendment to the U.S. Constitution, which banned slavery everywhere in the United States. Lincoln began making plans for **Reconstruction**, the process by which the southern states would rejoin the Union.

John Wilkes Booth (far right) shot Lincoln while the president watched a play at Ford's Theater in Washington, D.C. Mary Lincoln was sitting next to her husband when he was shot.

Mary Lincoln After Her Husband's Death

During the Lincoln family's years in the White House, Mary lost her son, her husband, and several family friends who fought in the Civil War. She had also lost another son, Eddie, before her husband became president. Mary never recovered from the tragedies she faced as First Lady. When Andrew Johnson moved into the White House to become the nation's next president, Mary quietly moved with her son Robert to Illinois. She later spent time in Europe before returning home to Springfield, where she died in 1882.

People noticed how old Lincoln was beginning to look. He had been leader of the country and of the North's military efforts during four stressful, difficult years. He had also lived through personal loss. His son Willie had died in 1862. His wife, Mary, was depressed throughout his presidency (and throughout the rest of her life). Pictures of Lincoln in 1865 showed a man who looked much older than he had in 1861.

Lincoln's Death

The Lincolns went to a play at Ford's Theater in Washington on April 14, 1865. Lincoln sat next to his wife in the presidential box—a section of the theater reserved just for them and their guests. An actor named John Wilkes Booth jumped into the box and shot Lincoln. Booth had supported the Confederates and hated Lincoln's ideas about ending slavery. The president was carried to a house across the street from the theater. He died the next morning.

Lincoln's body was taken by train to Springfield, Illinois. Millions of people gathered in cities along the train's route. They wanted to catch a glimpse of the president's body and say goodbye. Lincoln was buried in Oak Ridge Cemetery. Eventually, Mary and three of their sons were buried there, too.

Chapter 4

Designing and Building the Memorial

The country was shocked and saddened by Lincoln's death. Even people who had been critical of the president were deeply upset. In the years after Lincoln's death, there was some talk about building a memorial to honor him. Very little was done about it, however. The government did not have the money to build a memorial.

Plans for a Lincoln Memorial were finally discussed again in Congress at the beginning of the twentieth century. There were many questions to be answered: What should the memorial look like? Who should design it? Where should it be located in Washington? To answer these questions, Congress set up the Lincoln Memorial Commission in 1911.

Finding a Location

The commission members decided to place the Lincoln Memorial on the National Mall. They wanted it to run along the same line

This photograph shows the partially finished Lincoln Memorial building under construction around 1916.

as the Washington Monument and the U.S. Capitol building. The only problem with the location they chose was actually a big one—it was under water! The area was a **marsh** full of water from the Potomac River. It had to be filled in with soil to create dry land before the memorial could be built. Some people did not like this plan, including Representative Joseph Cannon from Illinois. He promised, "I'll never let a memorial to Abraham Lincoln be erected in that…swamp!"

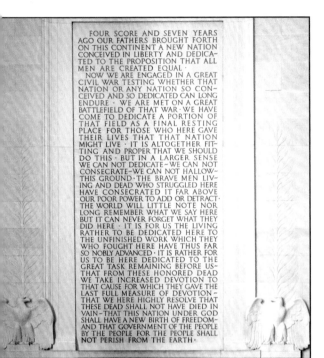

Lincoln's Gettysburg Address is on an inside wall of the memorial.

Designing the Memorial

In the end, the commission convinced Congress that the area by the Potomac River was the best place for the memorial. Next, the commission needed to find someone to design it. The members of the commission selected an **architect** named Henry Bacon. Bacon had studied architecture at the University of Illinois and in Greece and Italy. He had also designed some buildings for the Chicago World's Fair of 1893. He knew that he wanted the memorial to be full of symbols.

In Their Own Words

The Inscription over the Statue

There is an inscription over the statue of Lincoln inside the memorial. It says:

"In this temple, as in the hearts of the people for whom he saved the Union, the memory of Abraham Lincoln is enshrined forever."

The words were written by Royal Cortissoz, who was a close friend of Henry Bacon. Cortissoz was a newspaper writer who wrote about art for the *New York Tribune.* He later said that of all the things he had written during his lifetime, he was most proud of writing the words that appear inside the Lincoln Memorial.

Bacon designed a building that looked like a Greek temple. The building would be long, in the shape of a rectangle, and have columns, or supportive poles. There would be 36 columns to symbolize the 36 states that were part of the Union at the time of Lincoln's death. At the top of the columns are the names of the 48 states that existed when the memorial was constructed. (Because Alaska and Hawaii did not become states until 1959, their names today appear on a separate plaque.) Bacon also planned to have the words of two of Lincoln's most famous speeches—the Gettysburg Address and Lincoln's second inaugural address—appear on massive plaques on two inside walls of the memorial.

Next the commission selected an artist by the name of Jules Guerin to decorate the inside of the memorial. Guerin already had experience painting public **murals** in many buildings in the United States. He decorated the memorial with murals that were painted above the words of the Gettysburg Address and the second inaugural address. One

Lincoln's statue was carved in separate pieces, which were then put together inside the memorial.

mural shows scenes that symbolize the reunion of the North and the South after the Civil War. The other represents the emancipation of slaves.

The Statue

Bacon thought it was important to include a statue of Lincoln inside the memorial. A sculptor named Daniel Chester French was hired to make the statue. French made plans for a marble sculpture that would show Lincoln as strong and confident—the president who had led the country out of the Civil War. French created a 7-foot (2-meter) high model of the statue. He presented it to the members of the commission for approval. They liked it very much. The completed statue of Lincoln, which is 19 feet (6 meters) high, was placed at the very center of the memorial building.

The statue was actually carved by the Piccirillis—a family of six Italian-American brothers who worked under the direction of their father. They worked in New York. At 19 feet (6 meters) tall, the sculpture was much too large to be carved from a single piece of marble. There was also no easy

Segregation at the Dedication Ceremony

At the dedication ceremony for the Lincoln Memorial, Robert Moton delivered a speech. However, he sat away from most of the people attending the ceremony, in a separate section reserved for black people. Moton was the head of the Tuskegee Institute, an African-American college in Alabama. The college had prospered after emancipation, providing an education for former slaves and their sons and daughters. Moton respected Lincoln because he had ended slavery. Now, however, at the dedication of his memorial nearly sixty years after the end of the Civil War, black people were still kept apart from white people—a practice called segregation. The seating arrangement at the 1922 dedication ceremony showed that the United States still had a long way to go in terms of treating black and white people equally.

way of transporting the completed sculpture from New York to the memorial site in Washington. It was decided that the statue should be made of several separate pieces. The Piccirilli family completed the pieces in November 1919. They were then sent to Washington, where they were assembled. Then, French put the finishing touches on the statue.

Lincoln's son Robert (right) attended the dedication ceremony in 1922. At left is William Howard Taft. In the center is President Warren Harding.

The Dedication Ceremony

As the memorial neared completion, the country buzzed with Lincoln fever. It seemed that Americans had never before been more proud of Lincoln or remembered him in a better light. Thousands of people planned to attend a dedication ceremony to be held at the memorial on May 30, 1922. Robert Lincoln, the president's only surviving son, was also in attendance.

That day, William Howard Taft dedicated the memorial. Taft had been president when the commission was established, and he was now chief justice of the U.S. Supreme Court. Taft spoke to a crowd of about 50,000 people who had crammed onto the lawn in front of the memorial. Taft was quick to point out that, despite the deep respect being given to Lincoln, people had not always treated the president with so much respect:

"We like to dwell on the fact that his associates did not see him as he was when on earth, and that it was for generations, born after he was gone, to feel his real greatness and to be moved by his real personality."

Chapter 5

Visiting the Memorial Today

Thousands of school groups, vacationing American families, and people from other countries visit the Lincoln Memorial each year. These visitors are inspired by the things they learned about Lincoln in school or in history books. They come to the memorial to experience his words, to view the statue of him, and to see beautiful views of Washington, D.C.

When construction was completed in 1922, the Lincoln Memorial sat on a piece of land that seemed set apart from the rest of Washington. Since then, the construction of dozens of memorials and museums on or near the National Mall has changed the original setting. Today, memorials to presidents Thomas Jefferson and Franklin Roosevelt are nearby, as is the Washington Monument. There are also memorials honoring the veterans who fought for, and in some cases died for, the United States in World War II, the Korean War, and the Vietnam War.

The Lincoln Memorial and the dome of the Capitol building, which are at opposite ends of the National Mall, are both lit up at night. Between them is the Washington Monument. In the foreground is the Potomac River.

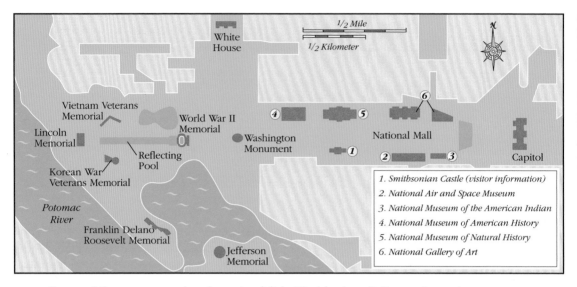

Some of the many popular places to visit in Washington, D.C., are shown here.

The Memorial Today

The memorial appears on American currency (money). It is pictured prominently on the back of the five dollar bill and the penny. These types of money both also show Lincoln's image. People visiting the memorial for the first time often recognize it because they have seen it on money.

Although the Lincoln Memorial was built more than 80 years ago, it retains an important place in American culture. In 1995, the Million Man March passed by the memorial as its marchers promoted African-American family values. In 2007, other marchers held a large-scale protest against the war in Iraq. The march began at the Lincoln Memorial.

In January 2009, a concert attended by tens of thousands of people was held at the memorial just before the **inauguration** (swearing in) of Barack Obama as the first African-American president of the United States. This historic inauguration took place exactly 200 years after Abraham Lincoln was born. It took place more than 140 years after Lincoln did so much to end African-American slavery in the United States.

The Lincoln Presidential Library and Museum

The Abraham Lincoln Presidential Library and Museum in Springfield, Illinois, is a more recent addition to the list of Lincoln historic sites. The library has many books and important documents concerning the president's life. The museum has several life-like exhibits meant to recreate events in Lincoln's life. Visitors can walk through rooms set up to resemble his boyhood cabin in Indiana, the White House kitchen, the room where Willie died in the White House, and even the room in which Lincoln's funeral service was held. Visitors can also see a copy of the only remaining photo of the president's body. The photo was taken at his funeral and was lost until it was rediscovered in the 1950s.

The "Lincoln penny" shows the Lincoln Memorial on the back.

Other Sites to See

For people visiting Washington, D.C., there are other places to see, in addition to the Lincoln Memorial, to learn about Abraham Lincoln's life and achievements. The National Museum of American History has many paintings, drawings, photographs, and objects related to Lincoln's life. Among many other things, the museum has tools that Lincoln used as a young man, a desk he used as a lawyer, campaign posters used when he ran for president, a suit he wore in the White House, a party dress worn by Mary Lincoln, and cups and other objects the

In Their Own Words

The Gettysburg Address

The Gettysburg Address is the speech that Lincoln gave at the dedication of the Gettysburg cemetery in November 1863. These words appear on the south wall of the Lincoln Memorial (the first words, four score, mean eighty):

"Four score and seven years ago our fathers brought forth, on this continent, a new nation, conceived in liberty, and dedicated to the proposition that all men are created equal. Now we are engaged in a great civil war, testing whether that nation, or any nation so conceived, and so dedicated, can long endure. We are met on a great battlefield of that war. We have come to dedicate a portion of that field, as a final resting-place for those who here gave their lives, that that nation might live. It is altogether fitting and proper that we should do this. But, in a larger sense, we cannot dedicate, we cannot consecrate—we cannot hallow—this ground. The brave men, living and dead, who struggled here, have consecrated it far above our poor power to add or detract. The world will little note, nor long remember what we say here, but it can never forget what they did here. It is for us the living, rather, to be dedicated here to the unfinished work which they who fought here have thus far so nobly advanced. It is rather for us to be here dedicated to the great task remaining before us—that from these honored dead we take increased devotion to that cause for which they here gave the last full measure of devotion— that we here highly resolve that these dead shall not have died in vain—that this nation, under God, shall have a new birth of freedom, and that government of the people, by the people, for the people, shall not perish from the earth."

Tens of thousands of people gathered to hear a concert at the Lincoln Memorial to honor Barack Obama on January 18, 2009—two days before he was sworn in as the first African-American president of the United States.

family used while Lincoln was president. In 2009, the museum brought many of these objects together for a special exhibit to mark the 200th anniversary of Lincoln's birth.

The museum also has a pocket watch that Lincoln owned. For many years, some people believed that there was some kind of secret message on the inside of the watch case. Finally, in 2009, the museum had an expert watchmaker open up the watch. And a message was found! Lincoln's watch was being repaired by a man named Jonathan Dillon on the day Fort Sumter surrendered. Dillon scratched a message onto the inside of the watch case that said in part: "April 13-1861 Fort Sumpter [his misspelling] was attacked by the rebels on the above date...thank God we have a government." It is believed that Lincoln never knew the message was there.

In Their Own Words

Lincoln's Second Inaugural Address

Lincoln gave his second inaugural address on March 4, 1865, when he was sworn in for his second term as president. At the time, the country was still fighting the Civil War. Lincoln wanted to encourage the Union to keep fighting. He also wanted to look forward to a time when the North and South would be reunited and living in peace. He did not believe that the southern states should be harshly punished after they rejoined the Union. The words from this speech appear on the north wall of the Lincoln Memorial:

"Fellow-countrymen: At this second appearing to take the oath of the presidential office, there is less occasion for an extended address than there was at first.... On the occasion corresponding to this four years ago, all thoughts were anxiously directed to an impending civil war. All dreaded it, all sought to avoid it.... Both parties deprecated [said they did not want] war, but one of them would make war rather than let the nation survive, and the other would accept war rather than let it perish, and the war came. One-eighth of the whole population were slaves, not distributed generally over the Union, but localized in the Southern part of it.... All knew that this interest [slavery] was somehow the cause of the war....

"Neither party expected for the war the magnitude or the duration which it has already attained.... Fondly do we hope, fervently do we pray, that this mighty scourge of war may speedily pass away....

"With malice [bad feelings] toward none, with charity for all, with firmness in the right as God gives us to see the right, let us finish the work we are in, to bind up the nation's wounds, to care for him who shall have borne the battle, and for his widow and for his orphans, to do all which may achieve and cherish a just and a lasting peace among ourselves and with all nations."

Visitors come from all parts of the United States and from around the world to see the Lincoln Memorial.

Another object in the museum's collection is the top hat Lincoln wore to Ford's Theater the night he was shot. Ford's Theater itself still exists and is now a museum. Visitors can see the box in which Lincoln sat on the night of April 14, 1865, and learn about how John Wilkes Booth plotted to kill the president. Performances are still held at the theater.

Honoring a Great President

Abraham Lincoln grew up in poverty but worked hard to reach the most powerful office in the United States. He believed in making life better for the common person, whether black or white. He worked to protect the rights of Americans at a time when they were being challenged by the practice of slavery. He reunited the country by defeating the Confederacy in the Civil War, only to die at the hands of an assassin. The Lincoln Memorial—with its stunning columns, life-like statue of the president, and location at the heart of the nation's capital—is a fitting, awe-inspiring tribute to one of the most respected American presidents.

Timeline ★ ★ ★ ★ ★ ★ ★ ★

★ **1809**   Abraham Lincoln is born in Kentucky on **February 12**.

★ **1816**   The Lincoln family moves to Indiana.

★ **1830**   Lincoln moves with his family to Illinois.

★ **1834**   Lincoln is elected to the Illinois state legislature.

★ **1837**   Lincoln opens a law practice in Springfield, Illinois.

★ **1842**   Mary Todd and Abraham Lincoln are married.

★ **1858**   Lincoln debates Senator Stephen Douglas about slavery, loses a Senate election to Douglas.

★ **1860**   **November:** Lincoln is elected president. **December:** South Carolina becomes the first state to secede.

★ **1861**   **February:** The Confederate States of America is formed. **March:** Lincoln is inaugurated as president. **April:** The Civil War begins at Fort Sumter, South Carolina.

★ **1862**   Willie Lincoln dies.

★ **1863**   **January:** Lincoln issues the final Emancipation Proclamation. **July:** Some 50,000 soldiers die in the Battle of Gettysburg, which is a major Union victory. **November:** Lincoln delivers the Gettysburg Address.

★ **1864**   Lincoln wins reelection.

★ **1865**   The Confederates surrender, ending the Civil War. Lincoln dies on **April 15**, one day after being shot by John Wilkes Booth.

★ **1922**   The Lincoln Memorial is completed.

★ **1939**   Marian Anderson, an African-American, sings on the steps of the Lincoln Memorial after not being allowed to sing at a Washington, D.C., concert hall.

★ **1963**   Martin Luther King Jr. gives his "I Have a Dream" speech on the steps of the Lincoln Memorial during the March on Washington for equal rights for African Americans.

★ **2009**   Barack Obama is sworn in as the first African-American president of the United States.

abolitionist: A person who supports or works for ending slavery.

architect: A person who designs buildings and other structures and who understands how they are built.

assassination: The murder of someone important, often a political leader.

civil rights movement: A movement during the 1950s and 1960s to achieve equal rights for African Americans.

convention: A large political gathering at which parties choose candidates for office.

debate: A discussion involving people with different views on the same issue.

emancipation: Freeing people from slavery or another unjust condition.

frontier: An undeveloped area of land on the edge of a settled area.

inauguration: The swearing in of a public official, such as a president, into office.

legislature: The part of a government that makes the laws.

marsh: Land that is wet or filled with water because it is close to a body of water.

memorial: A landmark or other place set aside because of its historic importance.

monument: A structure put up to remember a special person or event.

mural: A painting on a wall.

National Mall: A long, tree-lined plaza in Washington, D.C., that runs between the Lincoln Memorial and the U.S. Capitol.

plantation: A large farm; in the South before the Civil War, work on plantations was often done by slaves.

Reconstruction: The period of rebuilding after the Civil War, when the Confederate states came back into the Union.

regiment: An army unit; in the Civil War a regiment was generally made up of men who lived in the same state and sometimes even lived in or near the same hometown.

seamstress: A woman who sews for a living.

secede: To withdraw from, or leave, such as a state leaving the Union.

symbol: Something that stands for something else, often an idea or a place.

territory: A geographical area that belonged to the United States but was not itself a state.

Union: Another name for the United States.

To Learn More ★ ★ ★ ★ ★ ★

Read these books

Ashabranner, Brent. *A Memorial for Mr. Lincoln*. New York: G.P. Putnam's Sons, 1992.

Ford, Carin T. *The Battle of Gettysburg and Lincoln's Gettysburg Address*. Berkeley Heights, N.J.: Enslow Publishers, 2004.

Herbert, Janis. *Abraham Lincoln for Kids: His Life and Times with 21 Activities*. Chicago: Chicago Review Press, 2007.

Marcovitz, Hal. *The Lincoln Memorial*. Philadelphia: Mason Crest, 2003.

Ratliff, Thomas. *You Wouldn't Want to Be a Civil War Soldier! A War You'd Rather Not Fight*. Danbury, Conn.: Franklin Watts, 2004.

Look up these Web sites

Abraham Lincoln Presidential Library and Museum
http://www.alplm.org/home.html

Lincoln Bicentennial 1809–1865
http://www.lincolnbicentennial.gov

Lincoln Boyhood National Memorial
http://www.nps.gov/history/NR/twhp/wwwlps/lessons/126libo

Lincoln Memorial National Memorial
http://www.nps.gov/linc

Statues and Memorials: The Lincoln Memorial
http://bensguide.gpo.gov/3-5/symbols/lincoln.html

Key Internet search terms

Civil War, Emancipation Proclamation, Gettysburg Address, Abraham Lincoln, Lincoln Memorial, slavery, Washington, D.C.

The abbreviation *ill.* stands for illustration, and *ills.* stands for illustrations. Page references to illustrations and maps are in *italic* type.

Index ★ ★ ★ ★ ★ ★ ★ ★ ★

★ ★

About the Author

Chelsey Hankins grew up in central Illinois, where she often visited the Lincoln sites in Springfield on school field trips. She holds a B.A. from the University of Illinois, Urbana-Champaign, and an M.A. from The Ohio State University, both in American history. She lives in Chicago, where she works as a research editor and a freelance writer and fact-checker.